The Ghost in the Word

POEMS

Also by Arthur J. Stewart

Rough Ascension
and Other Poems of Science

Bushido: The Virtues of Rei
and Makoto

Circle, Turtle, Ashes

The Ghost in the Word

POEMS

by Arthur J. Stewart

Celtic Cat Publishing
KNOXVILLE, TENNESSEE

© 2013 Arthur J. Stewart

All rights reserved. No part of this publication may be reproduced, stored in a retrieval system, or transmitted in any form or by any means – electronic, mechanical, photocopy, recording, or other, except for brief quotations in written reviews, without the prior written permission of the publisher.

Celtic Cat Publishing
2654 Wild Fern Lane
Knoxville, Tennessee 37931
www.celticcatpublishing.net

We look forward to hearing from you. Please send comments about this book to the publisher at the address above. For information about special educational discounts and discounts for bulk purchases, please contact Celtic Cat Publishing.

Manufactured in the United States of America
Design by Dariel Mayer
Cover art by Justin A. Dickerman-Stewart; the design was inspired by Archie Ammon's poem, Easter Morning. Back cover photography by Lynn Freeny

ISBN: 978-0-9847836-9-4

Library of Congress Number: 2012954321

This book is for my "O" friends at Oak Ridge Associated Universities and Oak Ridge National Laboratory, who thrive on acronyms in their pursuit of science and science education. And, too, for all other scientists, engineers, teachers, and physicians who care about such things.

Contents

Preface and Acknowledgments	ix
Ambiguous Beginning	1
Where We Are	2
We Don't Know	4
All I Know	5
A Good Year	6
Back to Task	8
S&T	10
Going Off with Archie Ammons	11
Nothing Wrong	12
How Much	14
Starting Back to Work	15
From Archie to Japan and Almost Back	16
How Archie Ammons Did It	17
It Is So Easy	18
The Latest, Like Usual	19
Imagining It	20
Counting	21
What I'm About	22
I Don't Know Yet	23
Things Are Missing Everywhere	24
Evidence	26
Uncertain Mode of Ambiguous Discourse	28
Before the Wedding	29
Chupacabra	30
Wonderful Ways	31
Around	32
It's Nuts	33
Out the Ying-Yang	34
Working Group	35

A Hot, Dry Day	36
Poetry at the Roots of Science	38
Upon Diagnosis	39
Rest the Open Hands	40
Then and Now	41
In the Bleak Hours	42
Such Lament	43
When Someone Asks	44
Different Ways to Look	45
The Day Starts	46
What a Combination	47
Not an Aneurysm, Still a Worry	48
Friend	49
Day by Day, Night by Night	50
Which Way Is It	51
Deep in my Brain	52
One Day After	53
We Have	54
New Silk, Old Ways	55
State of the Union in Four Parts	56
Saturday Morning Review Job	58
It's All Better	59
Tick Tock	60
The Student Almost Glows	61
What Happened	62
The World Through Webcams	63
Crack in the Wall	64
After-Glow	66
What's Left	67
From One State to the Next	68
Bad Time of Year	69
Pausing, Near the End, by Lilacs	70
Notes	71
About the Author	73

Preface and Acknowledgements

In previous books of poems and essays, I thematically addressed, in succession, three ideas. The first of these was that scientists could benefit from becoming familiar with poetry and attending to their writing as a way to improve how they communicate science to the public (*Rough Ascension and Other Poems of Science*, 2003). The second idea, offered in *Bushido: The Virtues of Rei and Makoto* (2005), was that respect, truth and sincerity, both in science and daily life, are essential ingredients in advancing science due to their special importance in science education. These virtues, and several others, were associated with the Samurai warriors of Japan in the 1400s and 1500s, yet they pertain today. The third idea, advanced in *Circle, Turtle, Ashes* (2010), was that science education is itself an integral aspect of science: science stems from personal experience and is transferred in part to the next generation of scientists through parents, science mentors, and teachers. We cannot escape the personal aspects in such transfer, and there are in fact powerful reasons to understand and embrace personal aspects of science.

The central idea in *The Ghost in the Word* is to remind scientists, and poets, that ambiguity is the lifeblood and basis of both science and poetry. Science is pushing forward in multiple directions at an increasing speed, and the leading edges of this progression behave something like the leading edge of the cane toad invasion underway now in Australia: it is moving faster and faster through time, due to intrinsic evolutionary dynamics. As noted by Professor Rick Shine, who has worked extensively on the cane toad invasion problem, "evolution can happen simply because the fastest individuals always end up at the invasion front." The leading edges of science are pushing hard now into new territories of the unknown, the guessed-at and the not-understood, evolving as they go. And ambiguity is what these leading edges find, and what fuels them.

The leap-frog advances and heady twirls of insights spawned by science are not sterile intrusions of facts, and they do not yield pristine, perfectly formed technological products. Rather, the personalities of scientists seep into and affect their science, and the behaviors and attitudes of engineers creep into and shine from their wonderful technological advances. In fact, the idiosyncratic whims and notions of scientists and poets are central expressions of the creative process – and these whims and notions are far more important and valuable than generally recognized. The underpinnings of scientific and poetic endeavors depend on vision, perseverance, patience, logic, attention to detail, and creativity. Further, scientists and poets both apply these attributes daily to the same raw material – uncensored ambiguity.

Like other people, scientists and poets are ultimately drawn to their respective areas of work by the power of personal interest. Scientists and poets both have a personal desire to understand and explain, and they start with the same materials. However, scientists and poets "go after it" in different ways and they use very different tools. Further, the end products of scientists do not look much at all like the end products of poets, and certainly, the processes used by scientists to address ambiguity do not map one-to-one on the processes poets use to address ambiguity! Yet upon accomplishing an end product – a good experiment in one case, a thematically linked collection of poems in another – an odd and profound thing happens: scientists and poets both begin sharing what they have learned through their different modes of exploration. They begin communicating their results. By speaking and by writing, they begin expressing their findings, and in so doing they find commonality again – a jiggling, harmonic commonality of communication established by language.

When I first began considering ambiguity as the thematic backbone for this book, the idea seemed relatively straightforward. But my initial research on the topic of ambiguity quickly revealed multiple disturbing complexities. For example, according to Wikipedia, ambiguity in law is classified as either patent or latent, depending upon its source. Patent ambiguity relates to evidence explaining only what has been written, not what one intended to write, whereas latent ambiguity refers to evidence where wording is clear and intelligible, but may, at the same time, apply equally to two different things or subject matters.

Further, the military has established an acronym, VUCA, to characterize situations or conditions that are deemed volatile, uncertain, complex, or ambiguous. Then there's syntactic ambiguity – this term is used in describing sentences that can reasonably be interpreted in more than one way, or which can be interpreted reasonably to mean more than one thing. Syntactic ambiguity often can be alleviated by adding context. And finally, there's a large body of work on tolerance to ambiguity as a personality trait. A person with a high tolerance to ambiguity can readily perceive ambiguity in information and behavior, yet not become unduly stressed by it. Interestingly, tolerance of ambiguity seems to correlate with creativity, psychological resilience, lifestyle, orientation towards diversity, and leadership style.

Finally, language itself is inherently ambiguous. On this point, Lewis Thomas, in his book The Lives of a Cell, got it exactly right: "Ambiguity seems to be an essential, indispensible element for the transfer of information from one place to another by words, where matters of real importance are concerned." ... and "If it were not for the capacity of ambiguity, for the sensing of strangeness, that words in all languages provide, we would have no way of recognizing the layers of counterpoint in meaning, and we might be spending all our time sitting on stone fences, staring into the sun." The depth and breadth of ambiguity, both in science and language, initially set me on my heels.

But even while contemplating how best to develop the theme of ambiguity for this book, a personal VUCA situation emerged: I was diagnosed with prostate cancer. The trigger for this diagnosis was the result of a rapidly rising prostate-specific antigen (PSA) level – and at the time of my diagnosis, routine PSA testing was being hotly debated because PSA tests appeared to yield a moderately high rate of false-positive results. False-positive test results could trigger unnecessary treatment, which could needlessly increase medical costs. The core of this problem is simple: a PSA test is cheap, but it yields data of uncertain value. Increasing PSA levels are suggestive only – a definitive diagnosis of prostate cancer is made by biopsy and histological evaluation.

Not long after a biopsy confirmed that I had cancer, I underwent treatment by brachytherapy. But in the process of deciding upon the need for the biopsy, and in deciding upon the need for treatment following the biopsy, and in selecting the type of treatment after the results of the biopsy returned, I found unmitigated ambiguity aplenty. This ambiguity fused firmly with my anxiety and permeated into my writing. Cancer is scary. It also can push an individual to think hard about scientific things such as physiology, genetics, medical technologies, risk assessment, and statistics. For these reasons, I have distributed throughout this book a dozen poems that I wrote dealing with my own VUCA situation. These personal VUCA poems are sequenced in time, but are not aggregated into a separate section. The personal VUCA thread is one of several "ghosts" deliberately woven through this collection. Look carefully for the others!

Finally, I intend *The Ghost in the Word* to be enjoyable, whether or not the reader is invested deeply in science. So, while nearly every poem in this book contains some scientific or technological truth, each entry subjugates scientific points for greater reading pleasure. The Notes section, located near the end of this book, provides an avenue for accessing additional information relating to some of the poems.

Acknowledgments

I offer special thanks to Jim Johnston, for his keen attention to detail, superb editing skills, and unfailing sense of organization. His steadfast help has been a ten-year blessing. And I offer special heart-felt thanks to Monty Ross, my wife – she has graciously supported my efforts to combine science and poetry, through all four books, and kept me on a resolute course.

The Ghost in the Word

POEMS

Ambiguous Beginning

Recently I sensed
   a low-intensity, upper-
level disturbance: a weak perturbation,
a ripple, a small upset,

a nuanced quirk, a tiny odd-ball
out-of-the-ordinary
non-typical mismatch: in
short, a dinkle.

But that's

just how big things sometimes start – one
  teeny
    little
      thing
bumping another.

Where We Are

Up close, salmon-oil gel-caps have no smell;
they are the color of clover honey and slip down
easy with water and as they go I think
more about fish: a starry flounder
on a sandy bottom, two googly eyes peering up
from a one-sided face. Orange ruffe,
yellow-fin tuna, red snapper, silver-
sided grunion, blue hake.

In the world of water beyond thought
there's memory still. In Scotland,
salmon shimmer up falls in the river Shin,
hurling themselves
again and again, up
    and up, against gravity, against
the torrent of water roaring around rocks,
rainbows from the mist and spray, rainbows
as the fish muscle their way up
each year, year after year.

In the world of water, beyond thought,
250 million years ago
more than 90 percent of all species of marine animals
went extinct due to volcanic eruptions,
huge clouds of sulfur-gas, great blooms
of algae, drastic declines
in concentrations of dissolved oxygen.

Breathing in now, alive, I learn we live
in a three-second world – the average duration
of hugs, good-bye waves, musical phrases, the rate
of relaxed breathing, the length
of time for a handshake –
the duration of so many forgotten things
plugged in
as physiological fundamentals,
tight-wired in the brain. At night,

in labs, white rats stand
on their hind legs, their front paws raised
as if in supplication; they sniff
close-spaced bars in their cages like we sniff
the air when we enter
a new place from outside.

We Don't Know

So how big is a proton?
The answer is, we don't know: it is estimated

different ways by different teams of scientists,
and different ways

always yield different answers. Like
everything else, the answer depends

on the way the question is asked.

We don't know
the source of the Taos hum, or the place
where Big Foot lives, or how the sub-
conscious operates.

We don't know
what happened on the *Mary Celeste*, or
what's going on with UFOs, or understand
the mind-body connection, and

most of all we don't know
what we don't know.

All I Know

Counts as illusion: glitter
from hard light on sand or hiss
of wave on sand, or ripple of sand
under the water and here invest
in an abrupt muscle-twitch to fling
flat skip of rock above, counting
eleven, twelve
before it dives

    out there, out
of sight and mind,
the ghost in the word,
    having made
a small statement to the world,
exerting
force up, force down, forward
in the X direction an
intermittent breeze

ruffling for a moment the delicate
hairs on the arm, the surface
of the water, the skin
between this thing and that, oh,

such a thin
yet flagrant separation: I am

off to the lighthouse, not
by boat, but by the long walk,
one step at a time,
feeling the shore.

A Good Year

It's been a good year
for cholera, dengue fever, west Nile virus,
equine encephalitis and Ebola, and

bird flu keeps cooking along in
Thailand, Vietnam, Malaysia,
Indonesia, Egypt and

new things are stewing still
in the tropics,
moving out and up and now

even crop plants are taking hits:
by dark they sleep
with one eye open. What else

should I bring to your attention – a
gumminess of being, the sense of slogging
through work untangling

opinions from facts. Yesterday,
while driving home from work I learned
by phone our local high school football game

was drawing in
traffic to beat the band and clogging
roads to home like mad: the wife advised

a better route so I slithered
small roads a back way, ending up
just right, untaxed by need-

less clutter, that's fine. I discovered
later that night a new study of
coherent patterns in fluid flows

showing air-borne pollutants aggregate in
urban habitats in response to wind and this study
gives truth to the possibility of large-scale outdoor

feng shui, you can look it up.
And video games for predatory fish
shed light on the evolution of

group behavior and the movements of small
species that are their prey – see,
this does tie back

to what we do
or try to do
each day.

Back to Task

When the call came I was driving: I fished out
cell phone from pocket to learn
the number, something higher
than I had hoped for. What a loss
shall I become
to myself if a loss
to nothing else. So much
I've tried to do, so much
I've tried to get done even as

at home the Yoshino cherry has burst
to bloom and now, the morning after and yet before

    Easter morning, which I love,

the spring rain touches perfectly
the heads of the hyacinths, the bowed
shoulders of the peony blossoms hunched pink over
watching water spilling from sepals and
there is no perspective more perfect

than the I looking out,
though the peep-hole be small. To what
depth do we each extend,
by tendril or trunk, and to what aim? Such
questions are so far

beyond science, with its crystal lens and
edgy rules – even the negative
there has value: for example, reported today,
closing a hole in the heart is no better
than drugs in preventing stroke. And thankfully

in that domain one can always
leap sideways, plunge ahead to
safe unknown or fall to whimsy:
a new species of leopard frog, for example,
    found,

with its center of home range in
Yankee Stadium, the Bronx. But now

back to task:

re-toughen the self
to reality, who cares
to which axis of this multiplexed and
multi-variegated image of self
such effort pertains.

S & T

Amazing –
science is so much of us and yet is not

well thought of, or
thought of: it's out there unraveling

new tangles every day and we
forget about it

if we think about it
at all. Until, like Holub says in

Poem Technology, shit
something happened:

a reactor in Japan,
for example, behaves badly, coughing

up hairballs. But that's
technology going bad, the science

under the thing is solid, we know
the fission pathways, the amount of heat

released in each disintegration,
the distance on average that a

gamma ray goes before
puttering out in steel but

technology and science
are bedfellows, Mutt and Jeff,

they mix, not quite.

Going Off with Archie Ammons

He noted,
when nearly 70, stuff had bunched up

in his life and that's
just so right, it does: not clutter

quite but surely bunched
which makes me think

of bunch grass lizard – crafty little
Sceloperus scalarus, gotta love

the name and handsome thing,
 it lives

in the Chiricahua and Huachuca
Mountains in part but has been

in decline due to cattle-grazing, because
the lizard depends on bunch grass

for everything whereas cattle
depend on bunch grass

only in part, for food. Nothing
should go down like that: classify

the trend as a moral mistake
and you'll be kind.

Nothing Wrong

Nothing wrong with a wander – double-dose
the thing and   let   it   fly.

    Glare is a great book
of poetry, an ideal wander

tied up tight in strips and
try to do that if you can. In it

Archie's all over the map dissolving
the knot that clogs the pipe

that otherwise connects
this to that, one thing

to another. Last night
and this morning, too, the moon

was bigger than usual – bigger than
it has been for the past

    18 years, because

it was closer – orbital variance, but its
full-face mug shot

looked about the same
to me: it's difficult to see

a difference that small – to what
should you compare? Last month's

memory is no match for a
laser-based distance measure plus

calculated visual field and
besides, who cares? A hundred and twenty

or so cruise missiles
sleeked over water and

punctuated the air
defenses of Libya and even as they

did that, spent fuel rods housed
near the Japanese reactors continued

roasting as cooling water
leaked out, neutrons zinging

around like mad, and gamma
more than enough to fry eggs,

a little sparkle-dust on
spinach and fava beans, and in

milk – oh boy that
got attention – strange, people are so

sensitive about what goes in
their bodies in the form of food,

water, air; me too, it's as if
that's what really matters.

How Much

When the confirmation comes
at last it's
not news and I begin
a new phase – that of looking

deeply into the internet
and scientific literature for data
on what works and why
and especially, how well.

The confirmation triggers
a quiet rumble
of emails, low-level communications.
After all, how much
effort is reasonable to spend
for the self, the self being
    just one
of a multitude, with so much
need in the world and
not so much
special to offer?

Starting Back to Work

Hunched over my keyboard I'm writing
frizzled and frazzled. The desk is cluttered –

books, papers, business cards,
a cup of pencils and pens, a small box

of enigmas and questions which I save
for special occasions; three issues of

Science magazine – yes, I'm behind
again, but trying to rise

again, this time I'm planning to let
the mask fall, revealing

a gaunt face in a mirror looking back:
the hair is getting gray and wrinkles

crinkle the corners of the eyes and the eyes
look in more than they look out

    and what they see they send

whistling uncensored to the deep brain,
festering knot of slippery cells trying

to make sense of what comes in, in-
terpolating and extrapolating

data-bits like mad.

From Archie to Japan and Almost Back

He threaded his stuff on a strip
page after page, wish I

could do a thing like that and
off again, it's not over yet, things

will change: the sea-
floor earthquake that ripped Japan

several days ago was a big one, initiating
tsunamis – more than one

technically speaking, with the whole Earth
ringing like a bell

and if you were there probably
you, too, ringing like a bell but

just slippage, at its roots. We should know
better by now, she'll have her way and he

showed how he couldn't go
straight down the road

and there
you have it: the reactor

fizzing sea-water, and sea-water
having smashed what it could, now oozing

downhill back home, bricks
tumbling or sliding still

from where they were to new
locations of temporary

stability with aftershocks.

How Archie Ammons Did It

Sometimes he just rambled
for lines and lines, not saying much until

out of the blue, bang
he uncoiled

a snake, stepped back, looked
it over: diamonds, or mottled

like a copperhead or lean
as a racer, no need to poke

the thing with a stick, it's there
and that's enough – no eyelids, no

external ears, go ahead and count
the number of scales between the eyes.

It Is So Easy

It is so easy to forget
each thing
connects to another, item one

touches item three, two
there on the left,
far out, in direct contact

with item six and when
one moves, five moves, sometimes
slowly, sometimes

quick enough such that
the touch is evident and sometimes not

without a special look. And yet
the dipping buds of the Easter Lily in its pot
out back where the morning sun strikes first

tells a story of the story – did you know
it came originally from Japan and now comes
almost certainly from the Pacific Coast

having started three years ago and,
unfinished like that, prepare to recognize
it for what it is – a project: read

into it what you will, the mo-
lecular basis of what we need
day after day just to keep going:

virtue, innocence, hope and life. Consider
the lilies of the field, how they grow:
they toil not and do not spin and yet

like us, unfinished, end.

The Latest, Like Usual

The latest idea on the block
is this: when the universe was
before it was, it was

like liquid water and now
when we look back at it
to when we think

the Big Bang happened
thirteen point seven billion years ago
it cooled

just enough to crystallize into
what we see now: three dimensions
and time and theoretically

there should be defects
in the structure – so let's
  (harrumph)

get a grant to look for them.

Imagining It

My little friend
leans back, making himself
comfortable. He sips and sighs
a name I've not heard
anytime in my life; from that

special germling state of two
cells fusing to become one and that one
    dividing
over and over, making,
    at last, me, a squally
little red-faced creature with
eyes screwed tight
against light and, oh it took

such a long time before that little I
learned to love hard and
love light. Take this letter: Dear God

or whatever be your name, forward me now
that I am what I am. I've been made
from the thousands of choices I've made
since then to now and that

little friend with the dinkled
DNA takes another breath and he grows –
though I don't remember
inviting him in.

Counting

Each day I'm finding less
to thrash out and more
tangled ambiguity: everything's
snarled, caught up
in snares, complicated
by this thing or that. Sweet Jesus, the word if

wants to roll from the tongue pursuing
curves varied by muscular forcing of
puckered lips and such
distraction of self by self is so

mindless it stuns. Step back, re-
consider what needs inspection

really. One could say
a crocus times its spring-time splurge by
counting degree-days, silent,
eyes closed, underground.

What I'm About

According to Bukowski it's easy to slip
into the comfort of writing
clever poems devoid
of real emotion and guts,
and filling magazines with them,
making the magazines dull, pretentious and
unreadable and
sure, that happens. But life's
slippery as a salamander – a wet knife
goes in, comes out clean and
every day we get tangled in stupid little
situations, clogs, tie-ups, emotional

upsets, triangulations
where the three sides are
each different though the sum
of the interior angles, yes,
must be 180
degrees, so screw
his idea, maybe my work is clever but dull or
devoid of emotion and guts but
I work hard to get these little things
just where I want them: centered
on something that matters
to me.

I Don't Know Yet

quite what to make of it:
the dogs are friendly as ever, each one wags
like mad when I get home

    just like before

and Ladoga Lake and Nyos
was nominated for a Pushcart Prize
    but did not make the cut:
so many things I do
    don't quite
    make the cut.

Now lilies on our little pond out back
float on the dark water, opening
their blank faces to the sky,
each abrupt white
flower a surprise
even as
something grows
inside the gland – it needs
from my vantage to come out and

from its vantage
    it wants more
soft red dark.

Things Are Missing Everywhere

Astronomers toss at night worrying
about missing dark matter – an issue related
to the core-cusp problem, what a
lumpy discrepancy: could it be
due to temperature? Even a little warmth,
for example, and the smallest halos of matter
would not form, so the cusps would smooth.

Or perhaps all that empty space in space is
in fact filled
with weakly interacting massive particles – who knows?

Astronomers think they might need to weigh
the entire Milky Way – what a chore, but surely they could
take turns, fetching stars, one
after another. And such ambiguities
can't be helped, in any case – indeed, they help,
they grow the need for science.

In my office, behind my desk is my chair and
behind my chair, a floor-to-ceiling window.
It admits the light. There, just outside,
a little brown skink creeps
the sun and shadow-dappled ground, tilting
its head and looking
up and out with wary eye. His name
is *Scincella lateralis*. But I know
he doesn't know and doesn't care: he wakes
when he wants, he sleeps
when he chooses – no tossing there.

Damn it, where's the baryons?
They're modeled
at five percent of everything by mass but
  apparently
13.7 billion years gave them
time enough to hide.

Buried among the tangles of this
meander another problem lurks: the re-
union of ions in the universe.
The plasmonic tapestry
emerged from subtle initial irregularities
in the distribution of mass, and this allowed

electrons to be drawn to protons,
    and this allowed

early photons to skitter freely
from place to place through space but now

the mystery: when things cooled
much matter turned to light
    and then,   later,
some unknown input of energy intervened and
re-stripped atoms of their electrons leaving
a plasma in its wake.

I did not see my little brown skink
  today: he was missing, too, because
it grew cool,
    and cloudy,
        and then it rained.

Evidence

So little evidence is needed – much less
than one might guess. If,
for example, the full moon gives off
its own light, wouldn't the moon
be near-invisible when moving
across the face of the sun, light
against light? But no:
during a full eclipse of the sun
    one sees
only the sun's corona, its burning edge:
    the moon
by physical necessity blocks the sun's light.
    It blocks
the streaming rush of photons
released by fusion; the moon
does not glow by itself, it just reflects

light from the sun. What evidence
does one need to convince the self

not every word of any book should be
interpreted outside of the physical laws
we've found over the past
thousand years? The Mayans
worked up a fine calendar, the Incas left us

a mystery – from analyses of lead and silver
in lake sediments in the Bolivian Andes
      one can deduce
several thousand tons of silver were produced but
it is gone now. Where? Either it exists
hidden in a cave perhaps, or it
is gone, looted by later cultures. Eighty-four
thousand years ago people living in what is now
Madrid ate elephants and searching

within a scientific website this morning I found
two thousand three hundred and ninety one
hits for mystery.

Uncertain Mode of Ambiguous Discourse

On the matter of science one could say
the get-go is where it's at. For example:

Let's say you're studying plasmonics —
that is, density waves of electrons
created when light strikes
the surface of a metal under
special conditions: it can be
a powerful and flexible tool for probing
if you combine
super-hydrophobic artificial surfaces and
nanoplasmonic structures but

      light breaks free

when you try to confine it
to sizes below its wavelength
almost always, allowing

nanoscale quantum information processing
   some day
      maybe, probably,
(at the edge)
   we think.

Before the Wedding

Yesterday I got fitted
for a suit, a shirt and tie, a pair
of slick-bottomed patent-leather shoes,
a belt, such an

undesired situation by me, but fun
for the wife, she likes to shop while I
keep thinking, my god

    the amount

of dollars going into this vain
attempt to spruce an old man up would feed
50 Somali children for a year but
what then, I think: they might be fattened up
for awhile, maybe get old enough to pass on
their own set of squally genes and
there, we're right back to where we were

but worse. The entire concept
festers: I do everything I can
to stay civil while the guy has me

insert a finger between the tape
and neck to ensure good fit
of shirt around the throat. I pace
the room in the shining shoes,
I add a pleasant-sounding hmmm
while inspecting the held-up tie.

Chupacabra

I study a video of a purported Chupacabra –
the rear legs seem
longer than the forelegs, he's
mostly hairless, has large ears, substantial
cuspids and the tail is

extraordinary – long and hairless,
such that the overall
features of the creature are
distinctive, eye-catching, different. How long
before its DNA is
worked up, the animal's morphology and
physiology assessed, its breeding habits
and behavior reported in credible
scientific journals? Or how long
before it is discovered to be
a fox with mange?

The clock measuring the time-lag
between what is and what is
scientifically accepted
is ticking.

Wonderful Ways

There's so much happening, so many
　　things on fire:
bullets, branches, clouds
piling up in the west and winds
starting now to curl south, wave-crests
beating in time with the heart, one
after another, terrible things

in their relentless push and shove
against the land and of course

slow beauty, amongst these
the sort that pulls itself
up from the Earth, year after year, each
spring bringing new life, forgiving.

Inside me, I can sense
that little thing growing. It's not
malicious, it just wants to live; it is
lonely and confused. By taking over
a part of the body it knows

it will live at first, it will die, and
there's so many ways of bi-
furcating, day after day, so many

wonderful ways to go wrong.

Around

When we can't dig down we gaze up
looking
to name a thing we've not
noticed before, expecting of course
that by naming it we give it life and
by giving it life we extend
our own life or give life
meaning at least and

what the hell: it's so much
work to keep up with the crowd now as
its collective members pad
mile five of the ten-kilometer race, everyone
settling in a bit, the body knows
the pace at last, the repetitious
in and out of air needed to permeate
the lungs, the heart is a steady

hammer in the chest pushing the blood
through the tubes around
    and around
like thoughts.

It's Nuts

It is
difficult to slide
far from the self but that's
what needs to happen: that, then
turn back fast to look and if lucky see
pixilation – the tiny bits of light each
smaller than a dot, each too small to be any-
thing individually but together making
the picture whole. Like that: beads
threaded on a string of time and
time pixilated too, think about
it, it's really nuts: all this
empty space and we try
so hard to fit every-
thing into
  a nor-
  mal
 dis
t
r
i
b
u
t
i
o
n
.

Out the Ying-Yang

It's a warm day. We lean back in lawn chairs facing
away from the sun, in shade under
a massive maple; yes, hot, but sometimes a little
side-swipe of a cooling breeze. Rod said
to Ron: *best rinse that grease off or you'll have
yellow jackets out the ying-yang.*

The ying-yang. I thought about that
multiple times throughout the day
at rib-fest, with charcoal smoke
curling from multiple trailered-in grills:
twenty racks of baby-back ribs
tended by each team competing
for honor, trophy and
some small cash prize. What's
a ying-yang? It likely relates
to yin-yang, referring to

the all of everything, both sides,
relating, in short, to some
vast number. I dislike
the little bastards greatly, their
arrogant wobbly back-and-forth flight-path
low over the ground as they hunt
their territory, searching for meaty scraps.
A pint of gasoline poured down
their nest-hole at dusk does fine but
first you need to find the nest and
like life with luck you don't find it
accidently by stumbling over it
or else they'll get you good: sting you
out the ying-yang.

Working Group

In the business world today we met
around a table as a small group, just
small enough to get our pieces
said and then to get the said things
written down for review:
for up-scaling and informing
our managers as to what we think
is badly broken.

It is of course communication,
up and down, within and between
science education programs.
Lord help us, the protozoans
know how to do it and have done so
nicely for a million years.
How long will we work this pesky chore
trying and trying to get it right?

A Hot, Dry Day

This morning our preacher stretched
a parable a bit to fit
a truth in her head: water is
    she said
symbolic of life and death – I touch it
in my mind to my head in sign
of a cross. I listen to the story,
Jesus walking on water, Peter
losing his confidence
in his attempt to do the same and

calling out in fear for help

which came, and which should come
if all's right, if there is
no uncertainty: none.

But consider Werner Heisenberg,
whose father became
Professor of the Middle and Modern
Greek languages; the same Heisenberg

  who thought up

dead cats and live cats
and who sired seven children and
played Mozart and who became
iconic in the world of physics
after thinking alone

on Helgoland, rocky island in the North Sea
off the German coast and,
where others failed, succeeded
in ushering in

the golden age of theoretical physics –
   yet,
    what if
none of this is true?

Poetry at the Roots of Science

First two words begin rubbing
against one another, creating
tension, theme, a condition, a thing,
    a vector

having direction and magnitude:

    a force moves the reader from this
place to that. But see

how science works –
    bricks
made from clay mixed
with water of ambiguity,

question on question, edges
shaved just so, answers
explained and justified, the
methods are stated clearly, baked hard,
inspected, stacked.

Then one new shoot,
a single slender sliver of green,
comes up between two bricks.

Upon Diagnosis

To my quiet little friend:

I will not sing you a lullaby or tell
a once-upon-a-time story or sprinkle
cinnamon and brown sugar on oatmeal

just
for
you.

No. I circle your being;
I respect you
but I am wary. Something

feeds you from my blood –
    how could I hold you
dearer than that?

Rest the Open Hands

I lean back, close the eyes, rest
the open hands palm down on
an open book, William Carlos Williams'
Selected Poems, hoping
intensity will ooze up
the arms, feed the heart – but

some adjectives, some ad-
verbs distract and a few
too many exclamation marks hang
the ends of lines, terminating them
as with a ball-peen hammer. Yet,
be gone such criticisms; dash

the pinch-faced pucker-up
of distain, the works
are fine: they stand as firmaments,
they sound
a rich piping of plenty.

Then and Now

    Back then,

running the mile at a night meet
I'd lean into the curves left
the straights were
long tunnels of light,
people in the stands
yelling go, run and
  I'd be breathing
in excellent time, arms
swinging just so, one
after another, the toes
reaching for the extra inch, one
stride following another,
eyes to the shoes on the feet
of the runner in front of me,
aimed at closing
stride by stride

    but now

jogging the weight up hill
before dawn
in our suburban neighborhood;
streetlights on the left, I find myself
breathing hard and counting
the soft circles of light; robins are starting
their sleepy-song of awake and
I'm throwing
myself into the future
    such as it is
or will be, things
shrinking behind me.

In the Bleak Hours

In the bleak hours at night,
one third of the devil's number,
I can't sleep: it alarms

me, what the hell
does high PSA velocity imply
with respect to

progression, long-term
outcome, a preferred choice
of treatment?

In the bleak hours at night
I read dozens of papers, looking
for light.

Such Lament

A thread of me rises smoke-
like, a tendril up-coiling from ashes of
possibilities. I am, it was, once they were
like the plural of me: a plentitude
that, rising as marsh marigolds rise
from chill muck through
cool water to warm air in spring,
grasping light and gasping
the first breath of air – I, they, we refused

Refused! to melt back down un-

pretentiously, refused to give back that
which was taken up to grow.
Rather, busying the self,
a dark rose of being, taking and
taking and taking enough to
have something like
36 million heart-beats per year
just to push the red cells around
and around, even to the smallest tendrils
up-coiling through the brain.

Such lament
by the self for the self
as it readies to go. Such lament

in discounting things
it saw, felt or held trembling
like a fawn unknowing even as
it looks in vain for things
it does not know, did not see, feel or hold
dear to the heart, or deeper still.

When Someone Asks

When someone asks, "How's
your family?" I'm thrown

for a moment to confusion:
does the question mean
    my family,
the one I grew up with,
as a youngster – sisters
brothers, mom, dad, aunts, uncles
and the like
far away or does it mean

    my family
now, my children
mostly grown and out, my wife
and step-sons,
the dogs and cat and
oh, such
over-interpretation: actually

they're just
checking, making nice, are things

more or less OK? Have you
personal news you'd like
to relate? I tell the brain quit

digging, the hole's
too deep already.

Different Ways to Look

Scientists are busy looking for
physical analogs of the biological world – how

for example, a pile of staples when agitated
by shaking at 30 Hertz stabilizes as a complex

function of pile-mass and length of staple leg – it's like
how army ants cling together in a mass to allow

their comrades to pass over a stream
via a living bridge. A few days ago

while walking around the pond at work I saw
    a pickerel

suspended in clear water
motionless between the stems of a lily and

a muskrat which
rippled the water, arched his back and slid from view.

The Day Starts

The day starts
with my badge forgotten: half-way
to work I remember it, make
a U-turn, head home to fetch it.

The day starts
with a mockingbird
in acrobatic warfare above the trees:
you can tell he's pissed off, he's so busy
giving a hard-flying crow the full what-for.

The day starts
a thousand times over, second by second,
one minute fusing to the next, day-
lilies lining the path, a pillbug
running lickety-split fast
across the sidewalk.

The day starts,
it does not reset, it re-
starts, it re-
starts, a thousand

thoughts, a million ways.

What a Combination

Bad assumptions, bad data, bad
physics and bad luck prevailed in preventing
good prediction of
future large earthquakes. We should know
by now: the sum of angles does not
make zero, the areas under curves

keep slipping, we fail repeatedly –

attention to records in the past will not
prepare us perfectly for the future.

Blast chilling pork loins makes the meat
much tougher compared to spray chilling:

this finding, too, was
unexpected. How much
uncertainty, change in view, ad-
justment in understanding can we
tolerate before blowing
something: a cork,
a kettle, boiler, reactor – things
won't scale, a gaggle of engineers
stand around in baggy pants scratching
their half-bald heads.

Not an Aneurysm, Still a Worry

I worry
    that little almond

 in the brain
puts out   takes in

trace levels of chemicals
that make me fear

    this, that,
the other. One smell

      like lilac

brings a long
   time-ago forward

into now
   whatever

      now is.

Friend

It's muggy warm and dark
except for streetlights
as I jog. No bird-song: they stopped
their early morning territorial

trilling as joyful adulations
months ago. It is
almost autumn now, I'm in
pretty good shape

with respect to cardiovascular
condition but
that quiet little friend
scares me now and then –

I know he grows, I think he gives
a smeary mindless grin.

Day by Day, Night by Night

It seems we grow
full of ourselves, and fuller,
from time zero to the day we leave –

    it doesn't matter
that the sunflower turns
its head to face the sun

or that the little brown bat
squints as he shakes
out his patagia at dusk to start
pinging moths and mosquitoes;
    he is changing
his social behavior
to survive.

    It doesn't matter
that the old opossum opens
his toothy mouth in a pink yawn thinking
beetles, a grub perhaps, surely a fig or two

from the fuzzy-leafed tree, the one holding
a new nest now of beautifully ugly
baby robins out back.

The moon
is a western sliver at first
but it changes too, night by night,
becoming rounder, lower in the east.

Which Way Is It

The pineal gland is the only structure
in the human brain that does not
occur as a pair,
generating through Descartes
two questions – what is

the relationship between mind and body and what is
the relationship between structure and function?

There are few clues
to the ghost in the machine: there's a chance

for the mind to emerge
from soft tissue and electricity only, manifesting
through microscopes, cameras, fluorescent stains,
sensitive oscilloscopes, NMRIs and
complicated things like that or

what the hell – millions of monarch butterflies

are infected with a debilitating protozoan parasite
we call *Ophryocystis elektroscirrha*; it
slows them down and kills many, leading to
scientific exploration of the pesky and curious

ways in which many kinds of parasites
modify the behaviors of their hosts.
But maybe that's just
my *Toxoplasma* speaking.

Deep in my Brain

    Among the pieces of the mechanical under-
pinnings of the world
as we know it – the struts and wires,
angled plate-braces, riveted canti-
levered arms extending from
what we know to where
we think we want to know next

    well, I say

cogitate on this: dear science,
some days you're not all
you're cracked up to be, I'm just
    about
        convinced.
Some situations
have a weirdness that won't clear
even after correctly subtracting out
all relevant interaction terms, even after
I put on an aluminum-foil hat or
knock on wood or step over
a crack so as not to break
a back and

the old antennae now are positively
buzzing, I feel some big thing rising –

a concern, an accident, a major flip-
flop of the Earth along a crustal line or
maybe someone in my family is
about to be in big trouble: muons or
weakly-interacting massive particles or

quarks or parts of quarks, some
dinky little things are jiggling hard
deep in my brain.

One Day After

Afterwards I take
my meds on schedule, I drink water
glass after glass, enough to drown a cod, it keeps
the urine trickling
through the catheter into the bag –
dark yellow towards orange, steady
more or less, at a rate of about
330 milliliters per hour. The prostate
is dying; it is getting
bombarded with a dose
of gamma rays imposed
by tiny ^{103}Palladium seeds inserted there
yesterday as I slept deep
under anesthesia. Today,

I loll at home loggy on the sofa, chin
scratchy with unshaved whiskers, harassed
by the constant burning urge to pee.

We Have

Just a certain number of
lifetime breaths. Small things
breath quickly and travel
not far, using up life

and larger things
breath more slowly, travel farther,
using up life. What are we

to make of such information? And what
to do about the inevitable
ringers: for example, the four-ounce
Artic Tern – black cap, red beak, red feet,

deeply forked tail, long-lived, it migrates
more than 44 thousand miles per year,
    breathing, I bet,
the whole time, the little heart racing

in a warm breast under feathers.

New Silk, Old Ways

Well, they've managed now to stitch
spider genes into silkworms,
so the silkworms spin spider silk –
wonderful stuff that's delicate yet strong.
And this clever trick allows
immediate commercialization possibilities
because the new silk can be made
the old-fashioned way.

The mandibles
of the caterpillars work
night and day on fresh mulberry leaves
and when old enough, each caterpillar
rears up, spins its cocoon
and begins its sleep

> just like they've done
> for a thousand years – at peace,
> dreaming

kimonos, not knowing
they'll soon be plunged
into boiling water this time to help make
military vests.

State of the Union in Four Parts

1.
More than a week later:
it's cooling down, now it's less
than half as toasty as it was –
that's the beauty
of a short-lived radioisotope. It's
so much better for sure, with
no catheter, no tubes or bags, but
things still ache downstairs
and it's a busty
bowl-of-oatmeal-plus-six-prune job
to set things right as rain. You can look
at it this way – at least
it overrules my desire
to give a weather report.

2.
Oh what a small series, oh what a time
for more studious contemplation!
One thing flies out, something else
flutters in, we snip, we snug. Katla
is getting active and someone found
children's finger-paintings
on walls in the Rouffignac caves in France,
with the most prolific artist
estimated to be a girl, five years of age
and some of the marks left there were
up high, or even overhead, indicating
the work of a child held up or riding
on the shoulders of an adult. And
by analyzing these picture we know
these teaching and learning sessions occurred
about thirteen thousand years ago.

3.
So on we go to crumpled sheets
of graphene, designed to retain
full functionality of the surface area
    so much desired
or to the multiple electrons
sent out by coupled quantum dots in response
to single photons, making it much easier
to produce efficient solar cells or
…what's this? An underlying order
has been revealed by imaging
quantum-correlated particle-hole pairs
in a gas of ultra-cold
rubidium atoms held just so
by beams of laser light. Well –

4.
We know some things for pretty sure.
I take my ciprofloxacin on schedule,
my phenazopyridine
as needed, it is primarily matters of the heart that hurt
    and I love
loving   so much, remember
pale green needles
of tall fescue are emerging
now from the seed tossed to the rough-raked
bare spots of the lawn last week and
already
the quick frog slips silent
from the pond's sunny edge to the perceived safety
of the water between the stems of the lilies,
already
autumn birds huddle in nearby trees
watching the feeder for a refill.

Saturday Morning Review Job

In spite of goes
to *despite*, *an experiment
was conducted* becomes
we conducted an experiment. Add

a hyphen where it belongs, between
five and milligram when the two words are used
to describe sample size, eradicate
the ambiguous pronoun, italicize
the genus name. Un-split
infinitives here and there; data are
by nature plural. Why not

break the paragraph? Put this part, e.g.,
in materials and methods, explain
experimental design so as to include
information about data transformation and the type
of statistical tests you used, explain

what you did with outliers,
how you checked for heteroskedasticity.
Completely reorganize
the discussion: start by putting

the most important point first.

It's All Better

Here I am writing, April, 2011.
It's morning again.

For calibration, this is month
one hundred and sixty-one of
documented filing of poems written
electronically, and snugged in
month-by-month folders.

That's almost
thirteen and a half years.
What's out there to show for it
is not that much.

I lean back a moment, thinking.
Archie did better, and so-and-so
has more books, or that person
has more fame and glory.

Then, I laugh.
It's all better, for outside I see
the dogwood has exploded white,
    amazing
against the green.

Tick Tock

Five months cancer-free
or, more correctly,
five months with no
evidence of its return.
So they say from
my blood analysis,

but I suspect with
all the damage caused to kill it,
some half-whipped cell bearing dinkled genes
has out-drifted from the destroyed city,
seeking somewhere else to hide.

The Student Almost Glows

He's a rising junior.
The university name eludes me now.
He tells me his mentor is

      like a god,

sending him for work done well,
to the American Geophysical Union's meeting,
two months from now in California where

      he has family.

How much these things count, you can tell.
He might even give an oral presentation
of his summer's work, but that's still

      up in the air.

Around a delicate smile,
he doesn't look at me, quite.
He looks slightly down,

      tracing thoughts

in his head,
letting them run
like stallions,

      seeking the future.

What Happened

Broke a tooth at gum-line
eating cherries—so fine in spring.

The assessment:
extract, replace with implant.

Step one, a partial, mostly for looks.
Step two, nitrous and Novocain and,

almost before I was ready,
he drilled in, pulled it out,

packed in some artificial bone,
stitched it up and just like that it was done.

What else is an aging scientist to do?
Graph the results? Look for controls?

For days, if days are days,
I took the meds. It healed.

The World Through Webcams

By webcams I can see it's raining now
in Lagos, Nigeria.

It's drizzling on a man walking behind a warehouse
in Accra, Ghana and

it's hot, in Antalya, Turkey, with
the Mediterranean Sea popping blue next door.

Overlooking Lower Gardiner Street, in Dublin, Ireland,
buses, cars and people hop in and out of view, while

on the corner of Mason and Davis in Chicago,
a squirrel crosses the street and a man walks a dog.

In Iceland, there is mist, but
Katla rises behind olivaceous hills, serene.

Crack in the Wall

Once I was in ascendancy, a kite tugging
or a buzzard run-hopping to take off.
Now, 200 seasons later
the sun is full except

later this week, a nearly full eclipse
is expected: just a little
ring of fire is supposed to peek
around the edges, and

here I am in decendancy –
a crack in the wall.

It is, at first,
    just enough to let in
moisture and dust – the body of a black ant,
some pollen, a crumb of leaf.
    But it grows

as a natural consequence
of frost-heave, the exploratory
behavior of a beetle, a drizzle of rain,
    the inevitable
dissolution of ions, stresses and strains
of heating by day and cooling by night.

What if
it did not? The Earth
makes room for us all.

From a peep-hole it grows
slow to the size of young girl's fist:
a spider, some moss, a congress
of protozoans days following a rain. Firm
push-down of root, push-up of
gnarled bent-over stem, dogwood
aims yet to flower. With
leaf-rot and soil, all things
resurrect: a riot of color, light-flash, smoky
life-lust, bang and thrust,
warm and hold. So
sing me, please,
I so long.

After-Glow

When these eruptions
in writing happen, I get scared – what if

afterwards, all that's left
in me is flat: no more

craggy cliffs, *Ponderosa* logs
to roll, just one small

six-lined blue-tailed skink
peering up.

What's Left

Scant matters much: we've both changed,
we've kept the same
small habits, scoring them deeper
in their tracks; we put down
mulch, dug holes
for plants and, when necessary,
for pets and watered them with tears
and we've done and done
those thousand household chores
that never finish: dishes, laundry,
vacuuming, dusting
even the tops of books crammed tight in shelves.
What's left
from here on out? Professionally
past prime, I can try to teach
some things I've learned, I can try
to love you more.

From One State to the Next

I shuffle up and hesitate before knocking
the doorjamb of geezerhood:

what do I have
justifying entrance? Hearing loss,

fading eyesight, a gimpy knee,
the start

of a little pot belly, a smudge
of fear

at having accomplished
so little despite time spent.

Bad Time of Year

Staring too long at a blank page
on a computer monitor
can damage the ego: the id
seeks escape, wants to run,
turns and finds itself
     confused.

Toss facts
out the window for a moment:
Christmas leans forward, resting
its hairy snout
on my shoulder. It breathes
gloomy air like death
into my face and in this
bad time of year when I sleep,
I sleep badly. Last night I dreamed

of an intensely radioactive
potato, which I had eaten.
   As it worked
its way through, doctors
followed its progress as a bright
red-orange glow by CAT-scan.

Could this mean, don't eat starches,
they'll mess you up – stick
to green leafy vegetables, eggs,
cheese and meats? Hell,
I have no clue about

     what to do.

Pausing, Near the End, by Lilacs

I pause my walk, take a little
sideways glimpse
of the world, the sun cracking
the east ridge still dark:

    a quick peek,
do not see
the calculus of what is,
the negative log
of what is not. And thus while not
seeing
the underpinnings
of what there is to see, I see

one good choice only –
give back, not take. And that
presents the problem. It's
in with air, and the scent of the lilac; in

with water, food, fiber
as shielding from the elements
and structure
as further protection from
cold, rain and excessive sun.

So what's
to give? A trickling stream
of wastes, entropy,
lower-energy constituents, and

    somehow

comprehensive love
of all, to all, from me.

Notes

Preface *pages ix and xi*
    Shine, R. 2011. Invasive species as drivers of evolutionary change: cane toads in tropical Australia. *Evolutionary Applications* 5:107-116.
    Thomas, L. 1974. *The Lives of a Cell: Notes of a Biology Watcher*. Bantam Books, Viking Press, New York, NY.

A Good Year *page 6*
    Tang, W., Knutson, B., Mahyalov, A., and R. Dimitrova. 2012. The geometry of inertial particle mixing in urban flows, from deterministic and random displacement models. *Physics of Fluids* 24(6), 18 pages. dx.doi.org/10.1063/1.4729453
    Ioannou, C. C., Guttal, V. and I. D. Couzin. 2012. Predatory fish select for coordinated collective motion in virtual prey. *Science* 337:1212-1215.

Back to Task *page 8*
    Ammons, A. R. 1986. Easter Morning. Page 106 in *The Selected Poems, Expanded Edition*. W. W. Norton & Company, New York.
    www.cnn.com/2012/03/17/us/new-york-frog-species/index.html (accessed 11/11/2012).

S&T *page 10*
    Holub, M. 2007. *Poems Before and After: New Expanded Edition*. Bloodaxe Books Ltd. 438 p.

Nothing Wrong *page 12*
    Ammons, A. R. 1997. *Glare*. W. W. Norton & Company, New York.

The Latest, Like Usual *page 19*
    Ellis, G. F. R. and T. Rothman. 2010. Time and spacetime: the crystallizing block universe. *International Journal of Theoretical Physics* 49:988-1003.

What I'm About *page 22*
    Bukowski, C. 2004. *The Flash of Lightning Behind the Mountain*. Edited by J. Martin. HarperCollins Publishers, New York. 297 pages.

Things Are Missing Everywhere   *page 24*
    Finalist, long form, 2012 contest, Science Fiction Poetry Association. www.sfpoetry.com/contests/12contest.html

Evidence   *page 26*
    Abbott, M. B. and A. P. Wolfe. 2003. Intensive pre-Incan metallurgy recorded by lake sediments from the Bolivian Andes. *Science* 301(5641):1893-1895.

Chupacabra   *page 30*
    www.youtube.com/watch?v=cISfCVdmUE8

Different Ways to Look   *page 45*
    Gravish, N., Franklin, S. V., Hu, D. L. and D. I. Goldman. 2012. Entangled granular media. *Physical Review Letters* 108. arxiv.org/abs/1204.6654

What a Combination   *page 47*
    Huff-Lonergan and J. Page. 2012. The role of carcass chilling in the development of pork quality. National Pork Producers Council, Des Moines, IA.

Day by Day, Night by Night   *page 50*
    Langwig K. E., et al. 2012. Sociality, density-dependence and microclimates determine the persistence of populations suffering from a novel fungal disease, white-nose syndrome. *Ecology Letters* 15(9): 1050–1057.

Which Way Is It   *page 51*
    Altizer S. M. and K. S. Oberhauser. 1999. Effects of the protozoan parasite ophryocystis elektroscirrha on the fitness of monarch butterflies (Danaus plexippus). *Journal of Invertebrate Pathology* 74(1):76-88.

We Have   *page 54*
    Bejan, A. 2012. Why the bigger live longer and travel farther: animals, vehicles, rivers and the winds. *Nature Scientific Reports* 2:594 | DOI: 10.1038/srep00594

New Silk, Old Ways   *page 55*
    Teulé, F. et al. 2012. Silkworms transformed with chimeric silkworm/spidersilk genes spin composite silk fibers with improved mechanical properties. *Proceedings of the National Academy of Sciences* Early Edition doi: 10.1073/pnas.1109420109

State of the Union in Four Parts   *page 56*
    Guthrie, R. D. 2006. *The Nature of Paleolithic Art*. University of Chicago Press, Chicago, Il. 520 pages.
    Endres, M. et al. 2011. Observation of correlated particle-hole pairs and string order in low-dimensional Mott insulators. *Science* 334:200-203.

About the Author

Arthur Stewart was born in Michigan City, Indiana, spending childhood in what is now the Indiana Dunes National Park. He also spent time in Arizona, studying biology and chemistry at Northern Arizona University. Later, after serving in the Peace Corps, he earned his PhD in aquatic ecology at Michigan State University. He did postdoctoral research on the toxicity of coal oil and shale oil at Oak Ridge National Laboratory (ORNL), then learned and taught stream ecology at the University of Oklahoma before going back to ORNL as an ecotoxicologist, group leader, and senior scientist. To pursue his interests in improving science education, Art earned his MS Ed at the University of Tennessee, Knoxville. Currently, he works as a science education project manager for Oak Ridge Associated Universities in Oak Ridge, Tennessee. He lives in Lenoir City, not far from the hubbub of Knoxville.

About Celtic Cat Publishing

CELTIC CAT PUBLISHING was founded in 1995 to publish emerging and established writers. The following works are available from Celtic Cat Publishing at *www.celticcatpublishing.net*, Amazon.com, and major bookstores.

Regional *Appalachian Tales & Heartland Adventures,* Bill Landry

Poetry *The Ghost in the Word: Poems,* Arthur J. Stewart
Exile Revisited, James B. Johnston
Revelations: Poems, Ted Olson
Marginal Notes, Frank Jamison
Rough Ascension and Other Poems of Science, Arthur J. Stewart
Bushido: The Virtues of Rei and Makoto, Arthur J. Stewart
Circle, Turtle, Ashes, Arthur J. Stewart
Ebbing & Flowing Springs: New and Selected Poems and Prose (1976-2001), Jeff Daniel Marion
Gathering Stones, KB Ballentine
Fragments of Light, KB Ballentine
Guardians, Laura Still

Fiction *The Price of Peace,* James B. Johnston
Outpost Scotland, Abbott Brayton

Humor *My Barbie Was an Amputee,* Angie Vicars
Life Among the Lilliputians, Judy Lockhart DiGregorio
Memories of a Loose Woman, Judy Lockhart DiGregorio
Jest Judy (CD), Judy Lockhart DiGregorio

Chanukah *One for Each Night: Chanukah Tales and Recipes,* Marilyn Kallet

Young Adult *Voyage of Dreams: An Irish Memory,* Kathleen E. Fearing

Children *Jack the Healing Cat* (English), Marilyn Kallet
Jacques le chat guérisseur (French), Marilyn Kallet
Twins, Tracy Ryder Bradshaw

Memoir *Being Alive,* Raymond Johnston

www.ingramcontent.com/pod-product-compliance
Lightning Source LLC
Chambersburg PA
CBHW071202090426
42736CB00012B/2426